Collins

easy le

Fractions and decimals
bumper book

Ages 7–9

Elizabeth Dawson
and Chris Parkinson

How to use this book

- Easy Learning bumper books help your child improve basic skills, build confidence and develop a love of learning.

- Find a quiet, comfortable place to work, away from distractions.

- Get into a routine of completing one or two bumper book pages with your child every day.

- Ask your child to circle the star that matches how many questions they have completed every two pages:

Some = half or fewer   Most = more than half

- The progress certificate at the back of this book will help you and your child keep track of how many have been circled.

- Encourage your child to work through all of the questions eventually, and praise them for completing the progress certificate.

- This book includes problem-solving questions. For this type of question, space has been left for your child's working.

Parent tip
Look out for tips on how to help your child learn.

ACKNOWLEDGEMENTS

Published by Collins
An imprint of HarperCollins*Publishers* Ltd
1 London Bridge Street
London SE1 9GF

© HarperCollins*Publishers* Limited 2017

ISBN 9780008212438

First published 2017

10 9 8 7 6 5

All images and illustrations are
© Shutterstock.com and
© HarperCollins*Publishers*

British Library Cataloguing in Publication Data.

A CIP record of this book is available from the British Library.

Authors: Elizabeth Dawson and
Chris Parkinson
Commissioning Editor: Michelle I'Anson
Editor and Project Manager: Rebecca Skinner
Cover Design: Sarah Duxbury
Text Design & Layout: Paul Oates and
Q2A Media
Production: Paul Harding
Printed in Great Britain by Martins the Printers

MIX
Paper from
responsible sources
FSC
www.fsc.org
FSC™ C007454

FSC™ is a non-profit international organisation established to promote the responsible management of the world's forests. Products carrying the FSC label are independently certified to assure consumers that they come from forests that are managed to meet the social, economic and ecological needs of present and future generations, and other controlled sources.

Find out more about HarperCollins and the environment at
www.harpercollins.co.uk/green

Contents

Fractions

1 Numbers such as 1, 2, 3, 10, 25 and 100 are whole numbers.
When counting, these numbers show how many 'wholes' there are.

1 pizza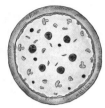

2 footballs

Sometimes amounts cannot be counted in whole numbers, so fractions are used.

How many pizzas are there? ☐

2 You will already know some fractions.

Match the fractions to their names.

$\frac{1}{2}$

$\frac{1}{4}$

$\frac{1}{3}$

one quarter

one third

one half

Parent tip
Make sure your child understands that $\frac{1}{2}$ means 'one of two' equal parts.

3 Fractions are made up of two parts:

The denominator (bottom number) shows how many equal parts the whole is divided into.

$\frac{1}{2}$

The numerator (top number) shows how many of the parts there are.

Circle the fractions with a denominator of 4.

$\frac{3}{4}$ $\frac{4}{10}$ $\frac{4}{5}$ $\frac{1}{4}$

Circle the fractions with a numerator of 3.

$\frac{1}{3}$ $\frac{3}{5}$ $\frac{2}{3}$ $\frac{3}{8}$

4 Here is a set of two cups.
What fraction of the set is shaded?

$$\frac{}{2}$$

5 Here is a set of four buttons.
What fraction of the set is shaded?

$$\frac{}{4}$$

6 Here is a set of objects.
Write the missing fractions.

◻ of the objects are ice lollies.

◻ of the objects are drinks.

◻ of the objects are ice creams.

Parent tip
Ask your child
'How many objects altogether?'
This will be the denominator
(bottom number of the fraction).

Halves and quarters

Halves and quarters are amounts less than one whole.

1 The fraction one half is written as $\frac{1}{2}$.

It means that the whole is divided into two equal parts.

Colour $\frac{1}{2}$ of each shape.

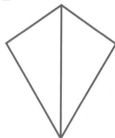 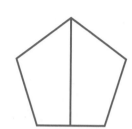 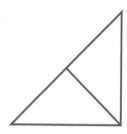

2 The fraction one quarter is written as $\frac{1}{4}$.

It means that the whole is divided into four equal parts.

Colour $\frac{1}{4}$ of each shape.

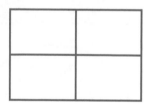  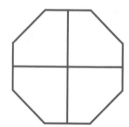

3 Tick (✔) the shape if it shows $\frac{1}{2}$. Put a cross (✘) if not.

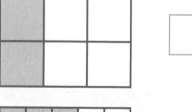 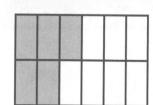

 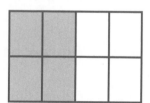

Tick (✔) the shape if it shows $\frac{1}{4}$. Put a cross (✘) if not.

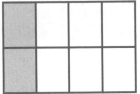

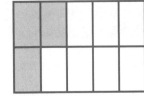

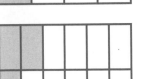

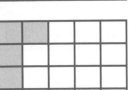

---

5 To find $\frac{1}{2}$, you divide by 2.

$\frac{1}{2}$ of 4 = 2 (because 4 ÷ 2 = 2)

Complete the number sentences.

$\frac{1}{2}$ of 10 = ☐ $\frac{1}{2}$ of 12 = ☐ $\frac{1}{2}$ of 100 = ☐

$\frac{1}{2}$ of 16 = ☐ $\frac{1}{2}$ of 20 = ☐ $\frac{1}{2}$ of 30 = ☐

$\frac{1}{2}$ of 40 = ☐ $\frac{1}{2}$ of 200 = ☐ $\frac{1}{2}$ of 50 = ☐

---

6 To find $\frac{1}{4}$, you divide by 4.

Complete the number sentences.

$\frac{1}{4}$ of 8 = ☐ $\frac{1}{4}$ of 12 = ☐ $\frac{1}{4}$ of 100 = ☐

$\frac{1}{4}$ of 16 = ☐ $\frac{1}{4}$ of 20 = ☐ $\frac{1}{4}$ of 40 = ☐

$\frac{1}{4}$ of 4 = ☐ $\frac{1}{4}$ of 400 = ☐ $\frac{1}{4}$ of 60 = ☐

Parent tip
To divide a number by four, you can halve it and then halve it again.

How much did you do?   **Questions 1–6**

Circle a star to show how much you have done.

 Some   Most    All

Thirds and fifths

1 The fraction one third is written as $\frac{1}{3}$.

It means that the whole is divided into three equal parts.

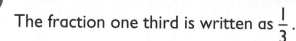

Colour $\frac{1}{3}$ of each shape.

 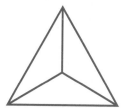 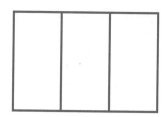

2 The fraction one fifth is written as $\frac{1}{5}$.

It means that the whole is divided into five equal parts.

Colour $\frac{1}{5}$ of each shape.

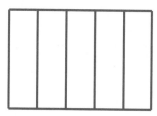  

3 Write the fraction that is shown by each shape.

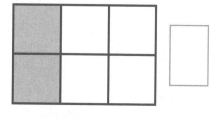 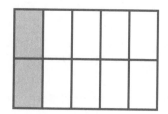

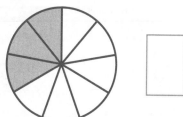 

Parent tip
Encourage your child to think about how many of the shaded areas would fit exactly into the whole.

1 Colour $\frac{1}{3}$ of the set.

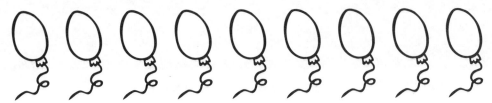

Colour $\frac{1}{5}$ of the set.

5 To find a fraction of any whole number, divide by the denominator (bottom number).

To find $\frac{1}{3}$ of 9:

$9 \div 3 = 3$

$\frac{1}{3}$ of 9 = 3

Use the example to help work out the answers.

$\frac{1}{3}$ of 3 = ☐ $\frac{1}{3}$ of 9 = ☐ $\frac{1}{3}$ of 6 = ☐

$\frac{1}{3}$ of 15 = ☐ $\frac{1}{3}$ of 30 = ☐ $\frac{1}{3}$ of 12 = ☐

6 To find $\frac{1}{5}$ of a number, divide by 5.

To find $\frac{1}{5}$ of 15:

$15 \div 5 = 3$

$\frac{1}{5}$ of 15 = 3

Use the example to help work out the answers.

$\frac{1}{5}$ of 10 = ☐ $\frac{1}{5}$ of 20 = ☐ $\frac{1}{5}$ of 15 = ☐ $\frac{1}{5}$ of 50 = ☐

How much did you do?   Questions 1–6

Circle a star to
show how much
you have done.

 Some   Most   All

Tenths

A tenth is 'one out of 10'. It is written as $\frac{1}{10}$. The whole is divided into 10 equal pieces.

Tick (✔) the shape if it shows a tenth. Put a cross (✗) if not.

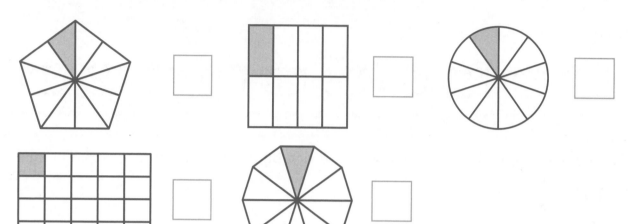

2 Colour the fraction.

$\frac{4}{10}$

$\frac{7}{10}$

$\frac{3}{10}$

$\frac{6}{10}$

$\frac{5}{10}$

3 How many objects are in the set?

What fraction of the set are:

tennis balls? $\frac{2}{10}$ footballs?   rugby balls?   cricket balls?

4 Draw a line from each fraction to the correct point on the number line.

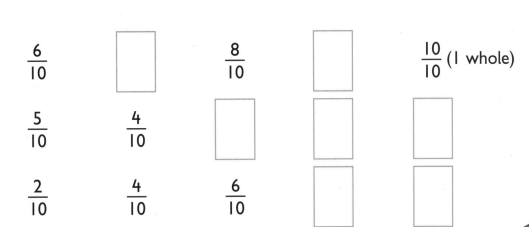

0   1

$\frac{2}{10}$ $\frac{6}{10}$ $\frac{1}{10}$ $\frac{5}{10}$ $\frac{9}{10}$ $\frac{10}{10}$

5 Complete each sequence.

$\frac{6}{10}$ ☐ $\frac{8}{10}$ ☐ $\frac{10}{10}$ (1 whole)

$\frac{5}{10}$ $\frac{4}{10}$ ☐   ☐   ☐

$\frac{2}{10}$ $\frac{4}{10}$ $\frac{6}{10}$ ☐   ☐

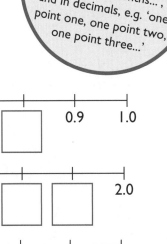
6 Another way of writing one tenth is **0.1**

Ones	.	Tenths
0	.	1

Fill in the missing numbers on the number lines.

0.0   0.1   ☐   0.3   ☐   ☐   ☐   0.7   ☐   0.9   1.0

1.0   1.1   1.2   ☐   ☐   1.5   1.6   ☐   ☐   ☐   2.0

2.0   ☐   ☐   ☐   ☐   2.5   ☐   ☐   ☐   ☐   3.0

Hundredths

A hundredth is 'one out of 100'. It is written as $\frac{1}{100}$. The whole is divided into 100 equal parts.

1 Colour squares on the hundred square to show the fractions.

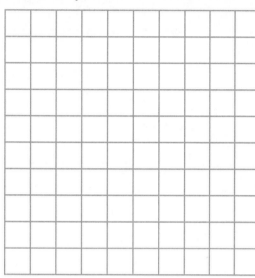

Red: $\frac{7}{100}$ Orange: $\frac{10}{100}$

Green: $\frac{3}{100}$ Blue: $\frac{5}{100}$

Parent tip
When colouring $\frac{10}{100}$ ask your child what they notice about the orange fraction. Point out that $\frac{10}{100}$ is equivalent (equal) to $\frac{1}{10}$.

2 Count on in hundredths. Write the next fraction in each sequence.

$\frac{2}{100}$ $\frac{3}{100}$ $\frac{4}{100}$ ☐ $\frac{21}{100}$ $\frac{22}{100}$ $\frac{23}{100}$ ☐

$\frac{78}{100}$ $\frac{79}{100}$ $\frac{80}{100}$ ☐ $\frac{45}{100}$ $\frac{46}{100}$ $\frac{47}{100}$ ☐

3 Count back in hundredths. Write the next fraction in each sequence.

$\frac{6}{100}$ $\frac{5}{100}$ $\frac{4}{100}$ $\frac{3}{100}$ ☐

$\frac{13}{100}$ $\frac{12}{100}$ $\frac{11}{100}$ $\frac{10}{100}$ ☐

$\frac{33}{100}$ $\frac{32}{100}$ $\frac{31}{100}$ $\frac{30}{100}$ ☐

$\frac{88}{100}$ $\frac{87}{100}$ $\frac{86}{100}$ $\frac{85}{100}$ ☐

4 Fill in the missing fractions.

$\dfrac{6}{100}$ $\dfrac{5}{100}$ ☐   ☐ $\dfrac{2}{100}$

$\dfrac{19}{100}$ ☐   ☐ $\dfrac{22}{100}$ $\dfrac{23}{100}$

$\dfrac{66}{100}$ $\dfrac{65}{100}$ ☐   ☐ $\dfrac{62}{100}$

$\dfrac{100}{100}$ ☐ $\dfrac{98}{100}$ $\dfrac{97}{100}$ ☐

---

5 To find $\dfrac{1}{100}$ of a number, divide by 100.

To find $\dfrac{1}{100}$ of 300:

$300 \div 100 = 3$, so $\dfrac{1}{100}$ of 300 = 3

Use the example to help work out the amounts.

$\dfrac{1}{100}$ of 200 = ☐ $\dfrac{1}{100}$ of 500 = ☐ $\dfrac{1}{100}$ of 700 = ☐

$\dfrac{1}{100}$ of 900 = ☐ $\dfrac{1}{100}$ of 1000 = ☐ $\dfrac{1}{100}$ of 400 = ☐

---

6 Write the value of each coin as a fraction of £1 (100p).
The first one has been done for you.

 $\dfrac{1}{100}$ of £1   ☐ of £1   ☐ of £1

 ☐ of £1    ☐ of £1   ☐ of £1

Parent tip
Give your child two or three different coins. Ask them to tell you the total value as a fraction of a pound, e.g. 22p = $\dfrac{22}{100}$.

How much did you do?   Questions 1-6

Circle a star to show how much you have done.

 Some   Most   All

13

Unit fractions

Fractions with a numerator of one are called unit fractions.

1 Draw a line from each fraction to its name.

$\frac{1}{2}$	one fifth
$\frac{1}{4}$	one eighth
$\frac{1}{5}$	one tenth
$\frac{1}{8}$	one quarter
$\frac{1}{10}$	one half

2 Write the fraction shown by each shape.

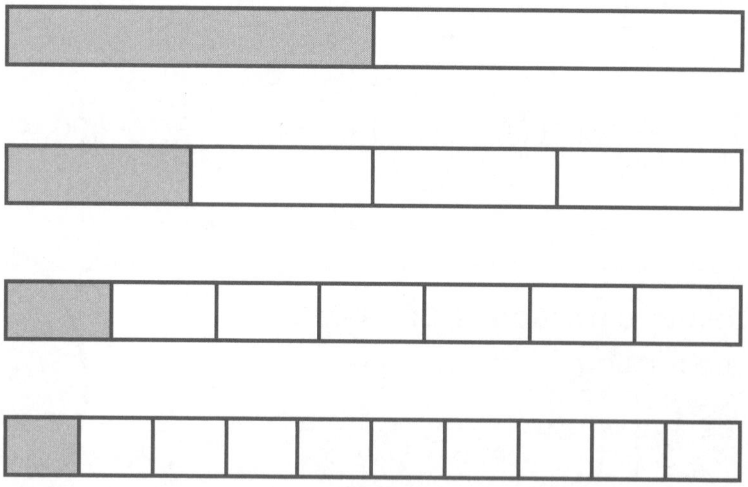

3 Write the fraction of white counters in each set.

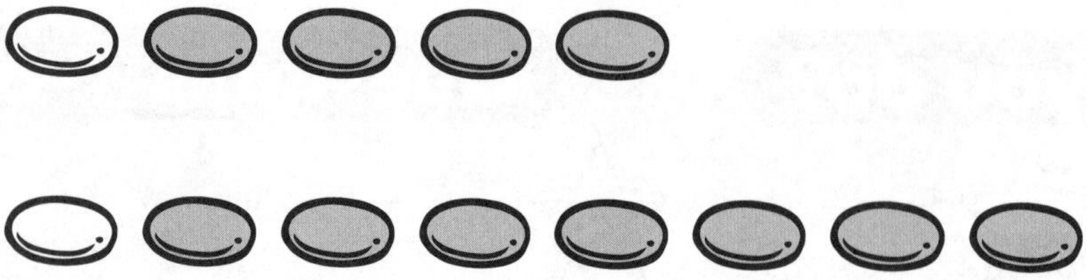

4 Draw a line to match each fraction to a shape.

$\frac{1}{5}$ $\frac{1}{6}$ $\frac{1}{8}$ $\frac{1}{9}$ $\frac{1}{10}$

  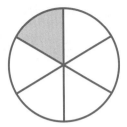  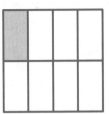

5 Complete the fraction wall.

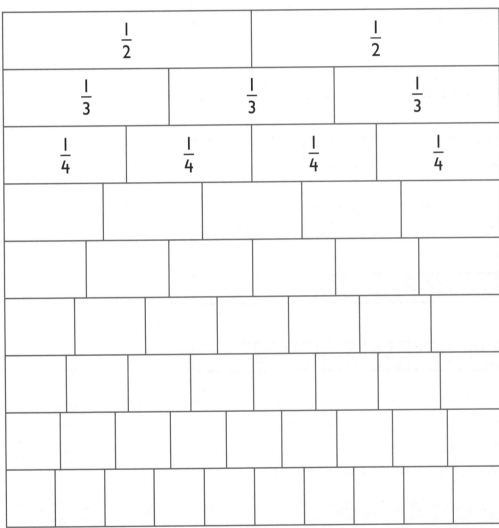

Parent tip
Encourage your child to count the number of parts in each row to find the correct denominator (bottom number).

How much did you do?   Questions 1–5

Circle a star to show how much you have done.

Some   Most   All

15

Non-unit fractions

Non-unit fractions have a numerator greater than 1.

1 Circle all of the fractions with a numerator greater than one.

$$\frac{1}{4} \qquad \frac{1}{2} \qquad \frac{3}{4} \qquad \frac{1}{7} \qquad \frac{2}{5} \qquad \frac{4}{6} \qquad \frac{1}{9} \qquad \frac{3}{10} \qquad \frac{1}{100}$$

2 This bar is divided into quarters.
Three of the quarters are shaded, so the numerator is 3.

$= \frac{3}{4}$

Write the fractions shown.

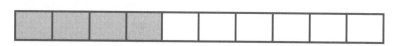

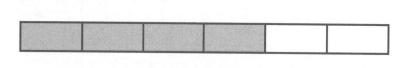

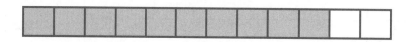

3 Count the different objects.
Write each amount as a fraction of the whole set.

Oranges

Apples

Pears

Bananas

4 Colour the fractions.

$\frac{3}{5}$

$\frac{6}{10}$

$\frac{3}{8}$

$\frac{5}{7}$

$\frac{5}{9}$

---

5 The fractions $\frac{1}{4}$ and $\frac{3}{4}$ add together to make 1 (a whole).

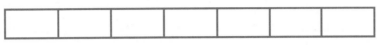

$$\frac{1}{4} \quad + \quad \frac{3}{4} \quad = \quad 1$$

Fill in the missing fractions.

$\frac{1}{10} + \boxed{} = 1$ 　　　　 $\frac{1}{8} + \boxed{} = 1$ 　　　　 $\frac{1}{5} + \boxed{} = 1$

$\frac{1}{3} + \boxed{} = 1$ 　　　　 $\frac{1}{6} + \boxed{} = 1$ 　　　　 $\frac{1}{100} + \boxed{} = 1$

---

6 Johnny has saved £30.

He knows that $\frac{1}{10}$ of this is £3, because he divided 30 by 10.

Work out how much of Johnny's money is shown by each fraction.

$\frac{1}{10} = £\boxed{3}$ 　　　　 $\frac{2}{10} = £\boxed{}$ 　　　　 $\frac{3}{10} = £\boxed{}$

$\frac{4}{10} = £\boxed{}$ 　　　　 $\frac{5}{10} = £\boxed{}$ 　　　　 $\frac{8}{10} = £\boxed{}$

How much did you do?　　　**Questions 1–6**

Circle a star to
show how much
you have done.

Some

Most

All

Comparing fractions

The more parts a whole is divided into, the smaller the parts.

1 The first circle in each row shows a fraction.
Colour the second circle to show a smaller fraction. Write the fractions shown.

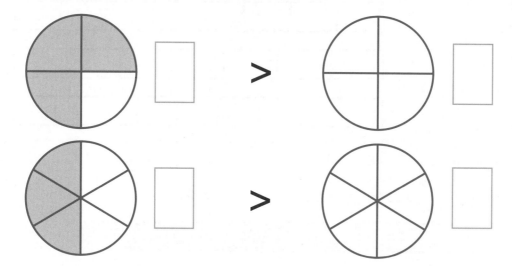

2 Write the fractions shown to complete each number sentence.

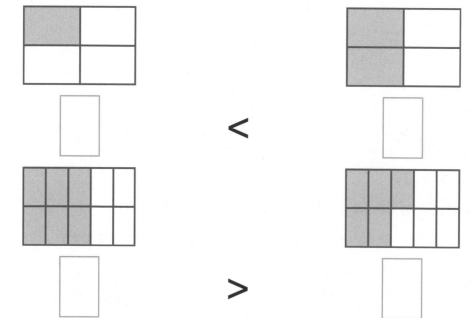

3 Tick (✔) the smaller fraction in each pair.

$\frac{3}{4}$ ☐ $\frac{1}{2}$ ☐ $\frac{3}{8}$ ☐ $\frac{1}{8}$ ☐

$\frac{1}{3}$ ☐ $\frac{2}{3}$ ☐ $\frac{2}{6}$ ☐ $\frac{4}{6}$ ☐

$\frac{1}{10}$ ☐ $\frac{1}{100}$ ☐ $\frac{2}{3}$ ☐ $\frac{3}{6}$ ☐

4 Write < or > in each box.

$\frac{2}{10}$ ☐ $\frac{8}{10}$ $\frac{46}{100}$ ☐ $\frac{47}{100}$

$\frac{3}{6}$ ☐ $\frac{2}{6}$ $\frac{9}{10}$ ☐ $\frac{10}{10}$

$\frac{99}{100}$ ☐ $\frac{1}{2}$ $\frac{4}{5}$ ☐ $\frac{7}{10}$

5 Circle the largest fraction in each row (going across the page).

$\frac{1}{10}$ $\frac{3}{10}$ $\frac{7}{10}$ $\frac{5}{10}$

$\frac{1}{4}$ $\frac{3}{4}$ $\frac{2}{4}$ $\frac{1}{2}$

$\frac{4}{8}$ $\frac{6}{8}$ $\frac{2}{8}$ $\frac{5}{8}$

$\frac{17}{100}$ $\frac{14}{100}$ $\frac{40}{100}$ $\frac{9}{100}$

6 For her homework, Samia has been using < and >.
Check her work. Put a tick (✔) if the number sentence is correct.
Put a cross (✗) if it is incorrect.

$\frac{3}{10} > \frac{2}{10}$ ☐ $\frac{1}{5} > \frac{4}{5}$ ☐

$\frac{5}{8} < \frac{6}{8}$ ☐ $\frac{1}{4} > \frac{1}{2}$ ☐

$\frac{3}{6} > \frac{2}{6}$ ☐ $\frac{1}{10} > \frac{80}{100}$ ☐

$\frac{4}{9} < \frac{3}{9}$ ☐ $\frac{5}{12} > \frac{3}{12}$ ☐

How much did you do?   **Questions 1–6**

Circle a star to show how much you have done.

Some

Most

All

Ordering fractions

Look at the numerators (top numbers) to help put fractions in order of size.

1

Fill in the missing fractions on the number lines.

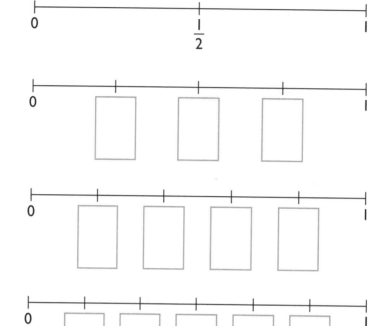

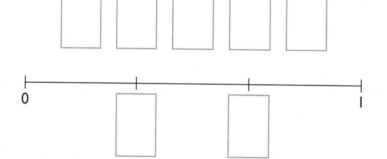

2   Put the fractions in order, from smallest to largest.

$\frac{3}{5}$ $\frac{4}{5}$ $\frac{2}{5}$

$\frac{9}{10}$ $\frac{6}{10}$ $\frac{10}{10}$

$\frac{9}{100}$ $\frac{19}{100}$ $\frac{2}{100}$

$\frac{4}{4}$ $\frac{1}{4}$ $\frac{3}{4}$

3 Below are the number of goals scored by players in a penalty shoot-out.
Each player takes ten shots at goal.
A prize is awarded to the player who scores the most goals.
Write the name of each player in the correct place on the results table.

Player	Goals scored
Josh	$\frac{7}{10}$
Sam	$\frac{2}{10}$
Mandeep	$\frac{5}{10}$
Paul	$\frac{8}{10}$
Bracken	$\frac{9}{10}$

Place	Player
1st (most goals)	
2nd	
3rd	
4th	
5th	

4 Circle the greatest amount in each row.

$\frac{3}{10}$ of a packet of sweets $\frac{7}{10}$ of a packet of sweets $\frac{5}{10}$ of a packet of sweets

$\frac{2}{5}$ of a carton of juice $\frac{4}{5}$ of a carton of juice $\frac{3}{5}$ of a carton of juice

5 Carla has seven cousins.

Sophie is $\frac{6}{12}$ of Carla's age, Ben is $\frac{8}{12}$ of her age and Jess is $\frac{1}{12}$ of her age.

Grace is $\frac{3}{12}$ of Carla's age, Alex is $\frac{4}{12}$ of her age, John is $\frac{9}{12}$ of her age and

Keith is $\frac{2}{12}$ of her age.

Put the children in order of their age, oldest first.

_____

Fraction word problems

1 Aisha, Sarah and Bela are playing with some marbles.
There are 32 marbles altogether.

$\frac{1}{4}$ of the marbles are pink. How many marbles are pink?

$\frac{1}{2}$ of the marbles are yellow. How many marbles are yellow?

2 There are 25 ducks on a pond.

$\frac{1}{5}$ of the ducks are brown. The rest are white.

How many ducks are brown?   How many ducks are white?

There are also 14 geese on the pond.

$\frac{1}{2}$ of the geese are male.

How many geese are male?   How many geese are female?

3 The table shows the scores in a dance competition.
Children need to score more than half to get through to the final.

Child	Score
Jamie	$\frac{4}{10}$
Stanley	$\frac{7}{10}$
Lucy	$\frac{1}{10}$
Rachel	$\frac{9}{10}$

Which children have made it through to the final?

4 Ben is given £4 and saves $\frac{3}{4}$ of it. Jeremy is given £10 and saves $\frac{1}{4}$ of it.

How much money has Ben saved?   £ ☐

How much money has Jeremy saved?   £ ☐

Who saved the most money?   _____

5 Altogether, Sally has £100! She keeps $\frac{1}{2}$ for herself.

Sally gives $\frac{2}{10}$ to her brother and $\frac{3}{10}$ to her mum.

How much money does Sally keep?   £ ☐

How much money does Sally give her brother?   £ ☐

How much money does Sally give her mum?   £ ☐

6 The children of Class 4 vote for their choice of class pet.
There are 30 children in the class.
Work out how many children voted for each pet. Complete the table.

Pet	Fraction	Number of votes
Guinea pig	$\frac{1}{3}$	
Fish	$\frac{1}{5}$	
Rabbit	$\frac{1}{10}$	
Hamster	$\frac{1}{6}$	
Dog	$\frac{1}{5}$	

Which pet was the most popular?   _____

How much did you do?   Questions 1–6

Circle a star to
show how much
you have done.

 Some

 Most

 All

Fractions equivalent to one half

Equivalent fractions are equal.

1   Tick (✔) the shape if the fraction is equivalent to $\frac{1}{2}$. Put a cross (✗) if not.

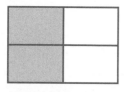

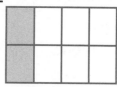

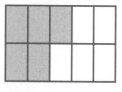

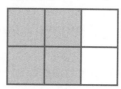

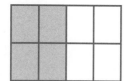

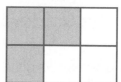

2   Colour one half of each shape. Complete the equivalent fraction.

Parent tip
Encourage your child to count the individual parts and name the fraction, e.g. there are eight parts, so one part is an eighth.

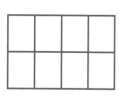

$$\frac{\square}{8} = \frac{1}{2}$$

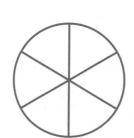

$$\frac{\square}{6} = \frac{1}{2}$$

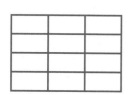

$$\frac{\square}{12} = \frac{1}{2}$$

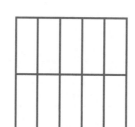

$$\frac{\square}{10} = \frac{1}{2}$$

3   You may have noticed something about fractions that are equivalent to $\frac{1}{2}$: the numerator is always half the denominator!

$$\frac{2}{4} \qquad \text{2 is half of 4}$$

Circle the fractions that are equivalent to $\frac{1}{2}$.

$$\frac{2}{6} \qquad \frac{4}{8} \qquad \frac{5}{10} \qquad \frac{2}{5} \qquad \frac{3}{12} \qquad \frac{10}{20} \qquad \frac{10}{50} \qquad \frac{4}{12} \qquad \frac{5}{100} \qquad \frac{5}{7}$$

Write the fraction shown. Put a tick (✔) if it is equivalent to $\frac{1}{2}$. Put a cross (✗) if not.

 Fraction   Equivalent to $\frac{1}{2}$

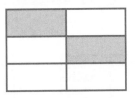

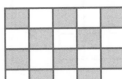

Complete the fractions to make them equivalent to $\frac{1}{2}$.

$\dfrac{3}{\square}$ $\dfrac{2}{\square}$ $\dfrac{\square}{10}$ $\dfrac{6}{\square}$ $\dfrac{10}{\square}$ $\dfrac{\square}{100}$ $\dfrac{\square}{6}$

Write the fraction and put a tick (✔) in the correct box. One has been done for you.

	Fraction	$= \frac{1}{2}$	$> \frac{1}{2}$	$< \frac{1}{2}$
	$\frac{3}{9}$			✔

How much did you do?   Questions 1–6

Circle a star to
show how much
you have done.

 Some   Most   All

Fraction families

Fraction families are groups of fractions that are equivalent.

1 Write the pairs of equivalent fractions shown.

 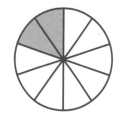 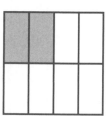

☐ = ☐   ☐ = ☐

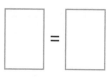

☐ = ☐

2 Colour the circles to show the equivalent fractions.

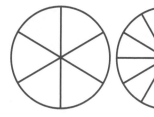  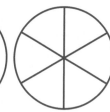 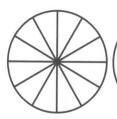

$\dfrac{2}{6}$ = $\dfrac{4}{12}$ $\dfrac{2}{3}$ = $\dfrac{4}{6}$ $\dfrac{8}{12}$ = $\dfrac{4}{6}$

3 To simplify a fraction, divide the numerator and the denominator by the same number.

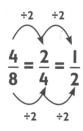

$\dfrac{4}{8} = \dfrac{2}{4} = \dfrac{1}{2}$

Parent tip
Remind your child that they must divide the numerator and denominator by the same number.

Simplify the fractions.

$\dfrac{2}{10} = \dfrac{\boxed{}}{5}$ $\dfrac{2}{6} = \dfrac{\boxed{}}{3}$ $\dfrac{5}{20} = \dfrac{1}{\boxed{}}$ $\dfrac{10}{30} = \dfrac{\boxed{}}{\boxed{}}$

4 Use the fraction wall to help fill in the missing numbers.

$\frac{1}{2}$										$\frac{1}{2}$									
$\frac{1}{4}$				$\frac{1}{4}$					$\frac{1}{4}$					$\frac{1}{4}$					
$\frac{1}{8}$		$\frac{1}{8}$		$\frac{1}{8}$		$\frac{1}{8}$		$\frac{1}{8}$		$\frac{1}{8}$		$\frac{1}{8}$		$\frac{1}{8}$					
$\frac{1}{3}$					$\frac{1}{3}$					$\frac{1}{3}$									
$\frac{1}{6}$			$\frac{1}{6}$			$\frac{1}{6}$			$\frac{1}{6}$			$\frac{1}{6}$			$\frac{1}{6}$				
$\frac{1}{12}$	$\frac{1}{12}$	$\frac{1}{12}$	$\frac{1}{12}$	$\frac{1}{12}$	$\frac{1}{12}$	$\frac{1}{12}$	$\frac{1}{12}$	$\frac{1}{12}$	$\frac{1}{12}$	$\frac{1}{12}$	$\frac{1}{12}$								
$\frac{1}{5}$				$\frac{1}{5}$				$\frac{1}{5}$				$\frac{1}{5}$				$\frac{1}{5}$			
$\frac{1}{10}$		$\frac{1}{10}$		$\frac{1}{10}$		$\frac{1}{10}$		$\frac{1}{10}$		$\frac{1}{10}$		$\frac{1}{10}$		$\frac{1}{10}$		$\frac{1}{10}$		$\frac{1}{10}$	
$\frac{1}{15}$	$\frac{1}{15}$	$\frac{1}{15}$	$\frac{1}{15}$	$\frac{1}{15}$	$\frac{1}{15}$	$\frac{1}{15}$	$\frac{1}{15}$	$\frac{1}{15}$	$\frac{1}{15}$	$\frac{1}{15}$	$\frac{1}{15}$	$\frac{1}{15}$	$\frac{1}{15}$	$\frac{1}{15}$					
$\frac{1}{20}$	$\frac{1}{20}$	$\frac{1}{20}$	$\frac{1}{20}$	$\frac{1}{20}$	$\frac{1}{20}$	$\frac{1}{20}$	$\frac{1}{20}$	$\frac{1}{20}$	$\frac{1}{20}$	$\frac{1}{20}$	$\frac{1}{20}$	$\frac{1}{20}$	$\frac{1}{20}$	$\frac{1}{20}$	$\frac{1}{20}$	$\frac{1}{20}$	$\frac{1}{20}$	$\frac{1}{20}$	$\frac{1}{20}$

$\frac{1}{5} = \frac{2}{10} = \frac{3}{15} = \frac{4}{20}$

$\frac{2}{5} = \frac{\square}{10} = \frac{\square}{15} = \frac{\square}{20}$

$\frac{3}{5} = \frac{\square}{10} = \frac{\square}{15} = \frac{\square}{20}$

5 Look at the fraction wall.
How many other sets of equivalent fractions can you find? Write them below.

_____

_____

_____

Adding fractions

1

Fill in the missing numbers.
Add the fractions together to complete each number sentence.

$$\frac{\boxed{}}{4} + \frac{\boxed{}}{4} = \frac{\boxed{}}{4}$$

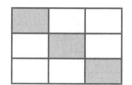 +

$$\frac{\boxed{}}{9} + \frac{\boxed{}}{9} = \frac{\boxed{}}{9}$$

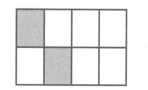 +

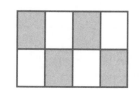

$$\frac{\boxed{}}{\boxed{}} + \frac{\boxed{}}{\boxed{}} = \frac{\boxed{}}{\boxed{}}$$

2 Add the fractions.

$\frac{1}{4} + \frac{2}{4} = \boxed{}$ $\qquad$ $\frac{2}{5} + \frac{2}{5} = \boxed{}$

$\frac{1}{3} + \frac{2}{3} = \boxed{}$ $\qquad$ $\frac{1}{6} + \frac{4}{6} = \boxed{}$

$\frac{7}{10} + \frac{1}{10} = \boxed{}$ $\qquad$ $\frac{14}{100} + \frac{18}{100} = \boxed{}$

3 Work out the missing fraction to complete each number sentence.

$\frac{1}{4} + \boxed{} = \frac{3}{4}$ $\qquad$ $\frac{2}{5} + \boxed{} = \frac{5}{5} = 1$ $\qquad$ $\frac{3}{10} + \boxed{} = \frac{7}{10}$

$\frac{1}{6} + \boxed{} = \frac{4}{6}$ $\qquad$ $\frac{2}{8} + \boxed{} = \frac{5}{8}$ $\qquad$ $\frac{18}{100} + \boxed{} = \frac{40}{100}$

4 Draw a line from each sum to the answer.

$\frac{1}{3} + \frac{1}{3}$

$\frac{2}{5} + \frac{2}{5}$

$\frac{1}{2} + \frac{1}{2}$

$\frac{3}{8} + \frac{2}{8}$

1

$\frac{5}{8}$

$\frac{2}{3}$

$\frac{4}{5}$

5 Fill in the missing fractions.

$\frac{1}{4} + \frac{1}{4} + \frac{1}{4} = \boxed{}$

$\frac{1}{5} + \frac{2}{5} + \frac{1}{5} = \boxed{}$

$\frac{2}{8} + \boxed{} + \frac{1}{8} = \frac{7}{8}$

$\frac{1}{9} + \frac{3}{9} + \boxed{} = \frac{6}{9}$

$\boxed{} + \frac{2}{8} + \boxed{} = 1$

6 Circle three fractions that add up to $\frac{7}{9}$.

$\frac{4}{9}$

$\frac{7}{9}$

$\frac{5}{9}$

$\frac{8}{9}$

$\frac{2}{9}$

$\frac{3}{8}$

$\frac{1}{9}$

How much did you do?

Questions 1–6

Circle a star to show how much you have done.

 Some

 Most

 All

Subtracting fractions

1 Complete the number sentences.

 —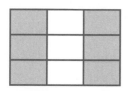

$$\frac{\boxed{}}{12} - \frac{\boxed{}}{12} = \frac{\boxed{}}{12}$$

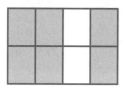

$$\frac{\boxed{}}{9} - \frac{\boxed{}}{9} = \frac{\boxed{}}{9}$$

 —

$$\frac{\boxed{}}{8} - \frac{\boxed{}}{8} = \frac{\boxed{}}{8}$$

$$\frac{\boxed{}}{6} - \frac{\boxed{}}{6} = \frac{\boxed{}}{6}$$

2 Subtract the fractions.

$$\frac{2}{4} - \frac{1}{4} = \boxed{} \qquad \frac{2}{5} - \frac{2}{5} = \boxed{} \qquad \frac{2}{3} - \frac{1}{3} = \boxed{}$$

$$\frac{5}{6} - \frac{2}{6} = \boxed{} \qquad \frac{9}{10} - \frac{3}{10} = \boxed{} \qquad \frac{78}{100} - \frac{64}{100} = \boxed{}$$

3 Fill in the missing fractions.

$$\frac{3}{4} - \boxed{} = \frac{1}{4} \qquad \frac{5}{5} - \boxed{} = \frac{3}{5} \qquad \boxed{} - \frac{3}{10} = \frac{2}{10}$$

$$\frac{5}{6} - \boxed{} = \frac{4}{6} \qquad \frac{4}{8} - \boxed{} = \frac{1}{8} \qquad \frac{40}{100} - \boxed{} = \frac{40}{100}$$

Draw a line from each subtraction to the answer.

$\frac{3}{3} - \frac{1}{3}$	0
$\frac{4}{5} - \frac{2}{5}$	$\frac{1}{8}$
$\frac{1}{2} - \frac{1}{2}$	$\frac{2}{3}$
$\frac{3}{8} - \frac{2}{8}$	$\frac{2}{5}$

Use all the fractions below to create two subtraction number sentences.
You can only use each fraction once.

$$\frac{5}{8} \qquad \frac{7}{8} \qquad \frac{6}{8} \qquad \frac{2}{8} \qquad \frac{3}{8} \qquad \frac{1}{8}$$

☐ – ☐ = ☐   ☐ – ☐ = ☐

Vinay has a bottle of cola.

After taking a drink, he has $\frac{4}{5}$ left.

Vinay then drinks a further $\frac{2}{5}$.

How much does he have left now?
Write your answer as a fraction.

☐

Decimal and fraction equivalents 1

1 Fill in the missing fractions on the number line.

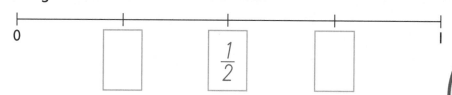

0   [ ] $\frac{1}{2}$ [ ]   I

Fill in the missing decimal numbers on the number line.

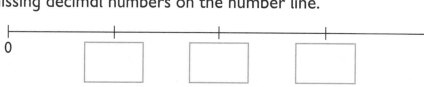

0   [ ]   [ ]   [ ]   I

Parent tip
Use the completed number lines to point out the equivalent decimal for each fraction, e.g. $\frac{1}{2}$ = 0.5

2 Match the fractions to the decimals.

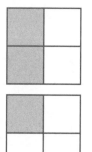

0.75

0.5

0.25

3 Write each amount shown as a fraction and a decimal.

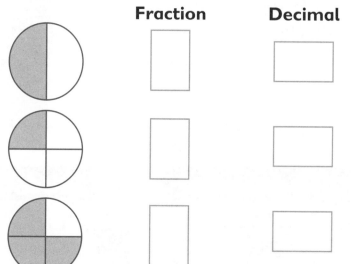

            Fraction   **Decimal**

Write the amount shown as a fraction and a decimal.

	Fraction	Decimal

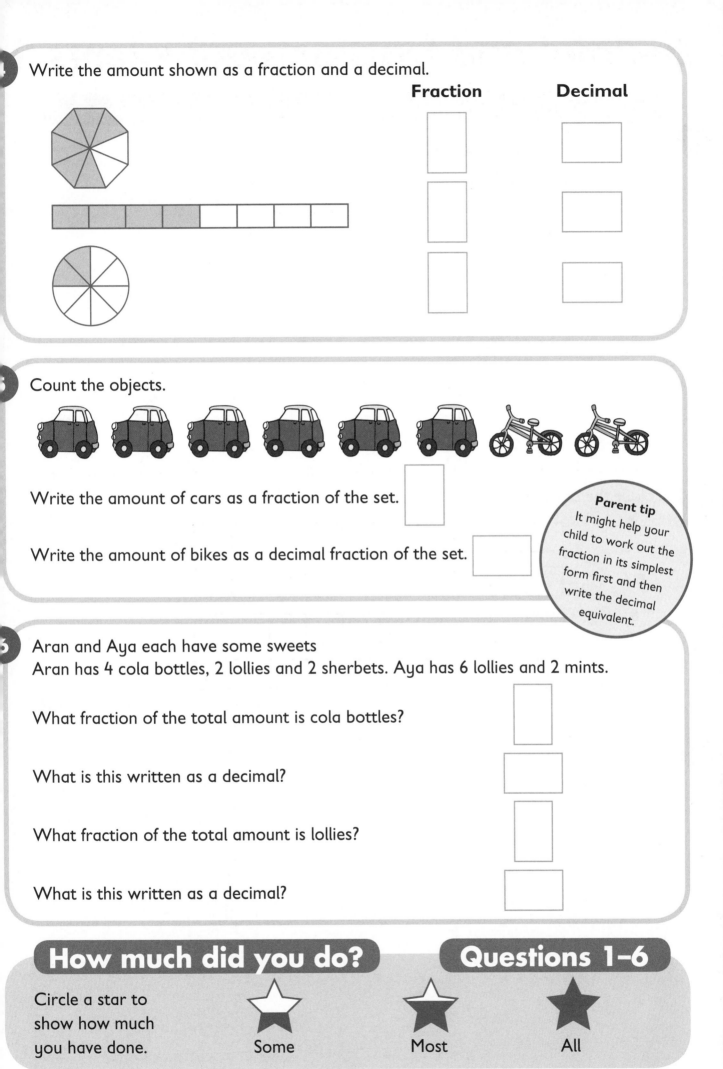

Count the objects.

Write the amount of cars as a fraction of the set.

Write the amount of bikes as a decimal fraction of the set.

Parent tip
It might help your child to work out the fraction in its simplest form first and then write the decimal equivalent.

Aran and Aya each have some sweets
Aran has 4 cola bottles, 2 lollies and 2 sherbets. Aya has 6 lollies and 2 mints.

What fraction of the total amount is cola bottles?

What is this written as a decimal?

What fraction of the total amount is lollies?

What is this written as a decimal?

How much did you do?   Questions 1–6

Circle a star to show how much you have done.

Some   Most   All

Decimal and fraction equivalents 2

1 $\frac{1}{10}$ is equivalent to 0.1, so $\frac{5}{10}$ (or $\frac{1}{2}$) is equivalent to 0.5

 $\frac{5}{10}$ (or $\frac{1}{2}$)

0.5

Write these fractions as decimals.

$\frac{5}{10} = \boxed{}$ $\frac{6}{10} = \boxed{}$ $\frac{4}{10} = \boxed{}$ $\frac{3}{10} = \boxed{}$

$\frac{1}{10} = \boxed{}$ $\frac{8}{10} = \boxed{}$ $\frac{7}{10} = \boxed{}$ $\frac{9}{10} = \boxed{}$

2 Colour the amount.

$\frac{6}{10}$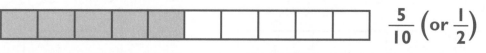

0.6

$\frac{8}{10}$

0.8

3 Draw a line to match each decimal to the equivalent fraction.

0.3 $\frac{9}{10}$

0.9 $\frac{3}{10}$

0.4 $\frac{7}{10}$

0.7 $\frac{4}{10}$

4 Fill in the missing numbers and fractions.

$0.\boxed{} = \dfrac{3}{10}$ $\dfrac{7}{10} = \boxed{}$ $\dfrac{2}{10} = \boxed{}$ $0.5 = \dfrac{\boxed{}}{10}$

$\dfrac{6}{10} = \boxed{}$ $0.2 = \boxed{}$ $0.9 = \boxed{}$ $\dfrac{8}{10} = \boxed{}$

5 The decimal number 0.01 shows there are 0 wholes, 0 tenths and 1 hundredth.
It is equivalent to the fraction $\dfrac{1}{100}$.

Ones	·	Tenths	Hundredths
0	·	0	1

Parent tip
Encourage your child to look at the positions of the digits in decimal numbers using the place value table.

Write these fractions as decimals.

$\dfrac{13}{100} = \boxed{}$ $\dfrac{17}{100} = \boxed{}$ $\dfrac{28}{100} = \boxed{}$ $\dfrac{7}{100} = \boxed{}$

$\dfrac{94}{100} = \boxed{}$ $\dfrac{22}{100} = \boxed{}$ $\dfrac{6}{100} = \boxed{}$ $\dfrac{9}{100} = \boxed{}$

Write these decimals as fractions.

$0.93 = \boxed{}$ $0.15 = \boxed{}$ $0.71 = \boxed{}$ $0.26 = \boxed{}$

$0.91 = \boxed{}$ $0.04 = \boxed{}$ $0.38 = \boxed{}$ $0.09 = \boxed{}$

6 Colour squares on the grids to show the given amounts.

Red: $\dfrac{14}{100}$

Blue: 0.16

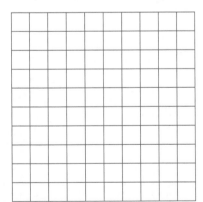

Red: 0.09

Blue: $\dfrac{11}{100}$

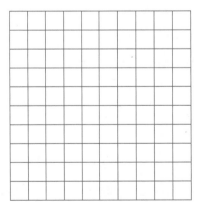

How much did you do?   Questions 1–6

Circle a star to show how much you have done.

 Some   Most   All

Counting with decimals

You can count in decimal numbers just like you do with whole numbers.

1 Fill in the missing numbers on the number lines.

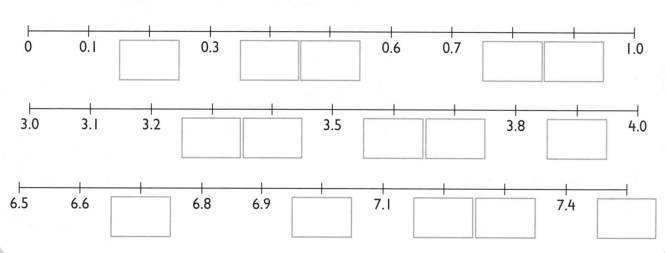

Number line 1: 0   0.1   ☐   0.3   ☐   ☐   0.6   0.7   ☐   ☐   1.0

Number line 2: 3.0   3.1   3.2   ☐   ☐   3.5   ☐   ☐   3.8   ☐   4.0

Number line 3: 6.5   6.6   ☐   6.8   6.9   ☐   7.1   ☐   ☐   7.4   ☐

2 Write the decimal numbers in order, from smallest to largest.

5.6	5.1	5.5	5.2	5.4	5.3
☐	☐	☐	☐	☐	☐

4.9	4.7	5.1	4.8	5.0	5.2
☐	☐	☐	☐	☐	☐

Parent tip
Practise counting in decimal numbers. Count forwards and backwards and across whole numbers, e.g. 1.9, 2, 2.1 …

3 Continue each sequence.

4.7	4.6	4.5	☐	☐	☐
3.1	3.0	2.9	☐	☐	☐
6.2	6.1	6.0	☐	☐	☐
9.3	9.2	9.1	☐	☐	☐
10.4	10.3	10.2	☐	☐	☐

4 Fill in the missing numbers on the number lines.

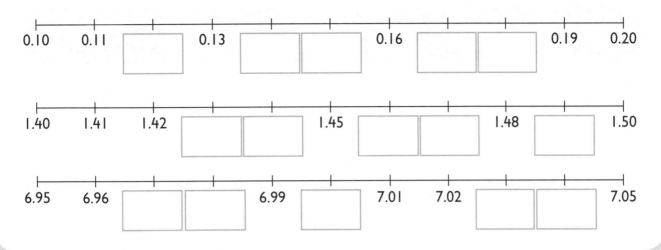

0.10   0.11   [ ]   0.13   [ ]   [ ]   0.16   [ ]   [ ]   0.19   0.20

1.40   1.41   1.42   [ ]   [ ]   1.45   [ ]   [ ]   1.48   [ ]   1.50

6.95   6.96   [ ]   [ ]   6.99   [ ]   7.01   7.02   [ ]   [ ]   7.05

5 Write these decimal numbers in order, from smallest to largest.

4.66	4.63	4.61	4.64	4.62	4.65
[ ]	[ ]	[ ]	[ ]	[ ]	[ ]

2.99	3.01	2.97	3.02	3.00	2.98
[ ]	[ ]	[ ]	[ ]	[ ]	[ ]

6 Continue each sequence.

3.16	3.15	3.14	[ ]	[ ]	[ ]
2.09	2.08	2.07	[ ]	[ ]	[ ]
1.01	1.00	0.99	[ ]	[ ]	[ ]
5.02	5.01	5.00	[ ]	[ ]	[ ]
10.91	10.90	10.89	[ ]	[ ]	[ ]

How much did you do?   Questions 1–6

Circle a star to show how much you have done.

 Some    Most    All

Dividing whole numbers by ten

When you divide a number by ten, all the digits move one place to the right.

1 Count the sweets and then share them between 10 people.
Draw rings around the sweets to show how many each person gets.

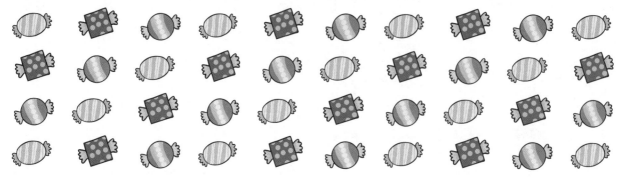

Fill in the missing numbers.

There are ☐ sweets altogether.

When shared between 10 people, each person gets ☐ sweets.

☐ ÷ 10 = ☐

2 Move all the digits one place to the right to divide by 10.
Write your answer in the place value grid.

60 ÷ 10 =

Tens	Ones	·	Tenths
	6	·	0

80 ÷ 10 =

Tens	Ones	·	Tenths
		·	

20 ÷ 10 =

Tens	Ones	·	Tenths
		·	

10 ÷ 10 =

Tens	Ones	·	Tenths
		·	

3 Divide these numbers by 10.

30 ÷ 10 = ☐

70 ÷ 10 = ☐

90 ÷ 10 = ☐

50 ÷ 10 = ☐

120 ÷ 10 = ☐

100 ÷ 10 = ☐

4 When you divide by 10, sometimes the answer is a decimal number.

$31 \div 10 = 3.1$

Circle the correct answer.

$22 \div 10 =$	2	2.02	2.2	22
$48 \div 10 =$	4.8	48	0.48	4.08
$96 \div 10 =$	6.9	9.6	9.06	9.66

Parent tip
Encourage your child to use a place value grid (like the ones in Box 2) if it helps them.

5 Divide these numbers by 10.

$42 \div 10 = \boxed{}$ $55 \div 10 = \boxed{}$

$29 \div 10 = \boxed{}$ $67 \div 10 = \boxed{}$

$99 \div 10 = \boxed{}$ $82 \div 10 = \boxed{}$

6 It is Helen's birthday and she is putting up balloons.
She has 10 balloons altogether and 96 centimetres of ribbon.

Helen needs to share the ribbon equally between the ten balloons.

How much ribbon does Helen need to cut for each balloon? $\boxed{}$ cm

Dividing whole numbers by one hundred

When you divide a number by one hundred, all of the digits move two places to the right.

1 Divide by 100. Write your answer in the place value grid.

$900 \div 100 =$

Hundreds	Tens	Ones	.	Tenths	Hundredths
			.		

$800 \div 100 =$

Hundreds	Tens	Ones	.	Tenths	Hundredths
			.		

2 Divide by 100. Write your answer in the place value grid.

$400 \div 100 =$

Hundreds	Tens	Ones	.	Tenths	Hundredths
			.		

$200 \div 100 =$

Hundreds	Tens	Ones	.	Tenths	Hundredths
			.		

3 Divide these numbers by 100.

$1000 \div 100 =$ ☐ $700 \div 100 =$ ☐

$500 \div 100 =$ ☐ $300 \div 100 =$ ☐

$600 \div 100 =$ ☐ $1200 \div 100 =$ ☐

4 When you divide by 100, sometimes the answer is a decimal.

   $482 \div 100 = 4.82$

Circle the correct answer.

$563 \div 100 =$	56.3	5.63	0.563	5
$124 \div 100 =$	1.24	124	12	12.4
$969 \div 100 =$	9	9.96	96.9	9.69

5 Divide these numbers by 100.

$242 \div 100 = \boxed{}$ $555 \div 100 = \boxed{}$

$629 \div 100 = \boxed{}$ $467 \div 100 = \boxed{}$

$899 \div 100 = \boxed{}$ $347 \div 100 = \boxed{}$

6 Fran has collected lots of one penny coins.
She knows that 100 one penny coins are equal to £1. $100 \times$ $= £1$

Fran counts all of her coins. Altogether she has 597 one penny coins.

How much money does Fran have in pounds?
Write your answer as a decimal number in the place value grid.

Parent tip
Reassure your child, that this question is the same as the ones in Boxes 4 and 5. They are dividing by 100 to find the answer.

Hundreds	Tens	Ones	·	Tenths	Hundredths
			·		

Fran's mum gives her another 145 one penny coins.
How much money does Fran's mum give her in pounds?
Write your answer as a decimal number.   £ $\boxed{}$

How much money does Fran now have in total?   £ $\boxed{}$

Decimals and money

1 Jamie buys a pen for £1.30 and a book for £2.50.
How much does Jamie spend altogether?

Parent tip
Encourage your child to think about the decimal numbers as fractions of one pound, e.g. £2.50 is two and a half pounds.

£ [ ]

2 At the school fair, Emily visits the cake stall.
Emily buys one slice of red velvet cake, one slice of Victoria sponge and a chocolate cup cake.

 £1.25   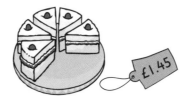 £1.45   50p

How much did they cost her altogether?

£ [ ]

3 Sara bought some football goals for her garden.
Each goal cost £23.50.
Sara bought two.
How much did the two football goals cost in total?

£ [ ]

4 Dillon buys two baseball caps.
Each baseball cap costs £4.25.

How much do the two baseball caps cost in total?

£ [ ]

5 Sarah spends £11.47 in a shop.
She pays with a £20 note.
How much change does she get?

£ [ ]

6 Raashid buys two pairs of socks and three T-shirts.

How much does Raashid spend altogether?

£ [ ]

How much did you do?   ## Questions 1–6

Circle a star to
show how much
you have done.   Some   Most    All

Rounding decimals

1

1.1 is closer to 1 than it is to 2, so 1.1 rounded to the nearest whole number is 1. If a number is exactly half way between two whole numbers, it is rounded up, e.g. 1.5 rounded to the nearest whole number is 2.

Look at the number lines and round to the nearest whole number.

```
|————————————————————↑———|
1                   1.9  2
```

1.9 rounded to the nearest whole number is ☐.

```
|———————↑————————————————|
3      3.3              4
```

3.3 rounded to the nearest whole number is ☐.

```
|——————————————↑—————————|
7             7.7        8
```

7.7 rounded to the nearest whole number is ☐.

2 Fill in the missing numbers.

1.4 rounded to the nearest whole number is ☐.

3.4 rounded to the nearest whole number is ☐.

4.5 rounded to the nearest whole number is ☐.

9.6 rounded to the nearest whole number is ☐.

3 The table shows the results of a singing competition.
The scores are rounded to the nearest whole number.
Work out which actual score belongs to each act. Choose from the scores below:

| 7.1 | 6.6 | 7.5 | 5.9 |

Results	Act	Actual Score	Rounded score
1st place	Eastlife		8
2nd place	Jessie G		7
3rd place	All Directions		7
4th place	Big Mix		6

4 Write **true** or **false** alongside each statement.

5.5 rounded to the nearest whole number is 6. _____

14.2 rounded to the nearest whole number is 15. _____

99.9 rounded to the nearest whole number is 100. _____

66.7 rounded to the nearest whole number is 68. _____

5 It can be useful to round numbers when estimating the answer to a calculation. Round the decimal numbers to the nearest whole number to estimate the answer.

4.5 × 5.1 ⟶ 5 × 5 = ☐

1.2 + 3.6 ⟶ ☐ + ☐ = ☐

9.9 × 9.8 ⟶ ☐ × ☐ = ☐

98.2 − 16.4 ⟶ ☐ − ☐ = ☐

6 Sally goes to the market. While her fruit and vegetables are being weighed out, she estimates what the total will be.

 Grapes: 1 kg for 50p

 Carrots: 1 kg for 40p

 Oranges: 1 kg for 50p

Sally's grapes weigh 0.9 kg.
Rounded to the nearest whole number that is ☐ kg.

Sally's carrots weigh 1.6 kg.
Rounded to the nearest whole number that is ☐ kg.

Sally's oranges weigh 2.4 kg.
Rounded to the nearest whole number that is ☐ kg.

Estimate the total cost for all of Sally's fruit and vegetables. £ ☐

How much did you do?   Questions 1–6

Circle a star to show how much you have done.

Some   Most   All

Comparing decimals

To compare decimals, compare every column starting from the left.

1

4.2 is 4 ones and 2 tenths. 4.1 is 4 ones and 1 tenth.

4.2 is larger than 4.1

Circle the larger decimal in each pair.

4.5	4.6		3.9	3.3
1.5	1.2		7.1	7.9

2 Write < or > to show which decimal is larger.

6.3 ☐ 6.5   4.8 ☐ 4.4

2.9 ☐ 2.7   6.2 ☐ 6.4

8.2 ☐ 8.5   5.7 ☐ 5.4

3 4.20 is 4 ones and 2 tenths. 4.16 is 4 ones, 1 tenth and 6 hundredths.

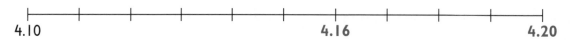

4.20 is larger than 4.16

Tick (✔) the **smaller** decimal in each pair.

2.30 ☐   2.25 ☐

4.70 ☐   4.66 ☐

3.10 ☐   3.11 ☐

5.60 ☐   5.99 ☐

4 Write < or > to show which decimal is larger.

2.21 ☐ 2.32   4.65 ☐ 4.68

7.12 ☐ 7.09   6.32 ☐ 6.35

5.12 ☐ 5.17   8.64 ☐ 8.46

5 Write **true** or **false** for each number sentence.

2.45 > 2.50 _____   6.31 < 6.40 _____

9.20 > 9.19 _____   4.40 < 4.46 _____

3.01 > 3.10 _____   12.01 < 21.10 _____

10.9 > 10.19 _____   7.77 > 7.07 _____

1.56 < 1.50 _____   8.16 < 8.61 _____

6 Put the decimals in order, from smallest to largest.

6.60   6.06   6.61   6.00   ☐ ☐ ☐ ☐

2.22   2.20   2.00   2.50   ☐ ☐ ☐ ☐

4.57   4.59   4.05   4.60   ☐ ☐ ☐ ☐

7.00   7.17   7.71   7.70   ☐ ☐ ☐ ☐

Decimals and measurement

1

2.1 cm

What is the length of all four sides of the square put together (the perimeter)?

[ ] cm

2 Aaron was 50.2 cm tall when he was 1 month old.
By the time he was 13, Aaron had grown a further 110.9 cm.
How tall was Aaron when he was 13?

[ ] cm

3 Jane decides it is time for a new haircut.
She goes to the hairdresser with hair that is 70.6 cm long.
When she leaves it is 20.3 cm long.
How much hair did the hairdresser cut off?

[ ] cm

4 A racing driver can travel at 100.15 miles per hour.
How far could they travel in 3 hours at this speed?

☐ miles

5 The legs on a table are each 30.2 cm long.

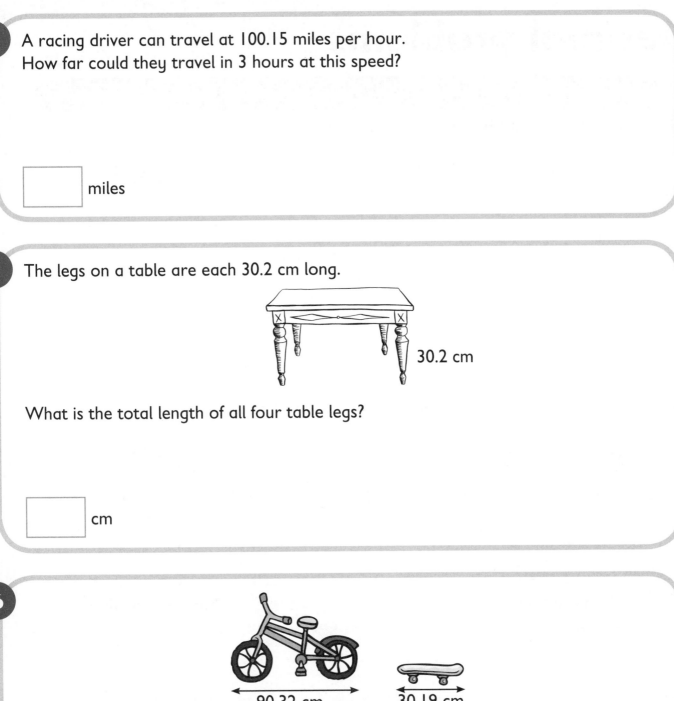

30.2 cm

What is the total length of all four table legs?

☐ cm

6

90.32 cm   30.19 cm

What is the difference in length between the two objects?

☐ cm

How much did you do?   Questions 1–6

Circle a star to
show how much
you have done.

Some   Most   All

Decimal problems

Solve the following problems, which involve decimal numbers.

1 Place the decimal numbers in the correct place on the number line.

| 0.1 | 0.5 | 0.75 | 0.25 |

0 ↑ ↑ ↑ ↑ 1

2 Put the prices in order, from least expensive to most expensive.

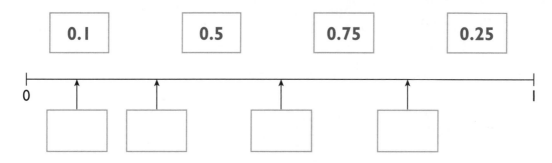

£1.20   95p   £4.99   £4.97

Least expensive   **Most expensive**

3 Complete the number sentences to show how each number can be partitioned. The first one has been done for you.

3.37 =   *3*   + *0.30* + *0.07*

5.64 = [ ] + [ ] + [ ]

7.63 = [ ] + [ ] + [ ]

9.92 = [ ] + [ ] + [ ]

12.29 = [ ] + [ ] + [ ] + [ ]

> **Parent tip**
> Remind your child that they are splitting the number into tens, ones, tenths and hundredths. They can draw a place value grid if it helps.

4 Choose a number to complete each number sentence.

| 1.3 | 2.2 | 5 | 10.8 | 7.2 | 4.5 |

3 + 4.2 = ☐   7 + 3.8 = ☐

4 + ☐ = 5.3   3 + ☐ = 5.2

☐ + 3.1 = 8.1   ☐ + 4.4 = 8.9

5 Choose a number to complete each number sentence.

| 9.8 | 3.2 | 7.0 | 6.2 | 0.8 | 2.5 |

8 − 1.8 = ☐   3 − 2.2 = ☐

7 − ☐ = 4.5   5 − ☐ = 1.8

☐ − 4.3 = 2.7   ☐ − 6.7 = 3.1

6 Use the numbers to make two number sentences.
You can only use each number once.

| 2.1 | 2.4 | 5.3 | 5.5 | 3.2 | 3.1 |

☐ + ☐ = ☐

☐ − ☐ = ☐

Fractions and measurement

1 Alisha is 160 cm tall. Her brother is $\frac{1}{2}$ her height.
How tall is Alisha's brother?

[ ] cm

2 The weather forecast says that it will be 20°C in London.
Fill in the temperature for each of the other cities.

Glasgow: $\frac{1}{10}$ the temperature of London

York: $\frac{1}{2}$ the temperature of London

Newquay: $\frac{1}{4}$ the temperature of London

London: 20°C

York [ ] °C   Glasgow [ ] °C   Newquay [ ] °C

3 Calculate the fractions of each quantity to complete the table.

	$\frac{1}{4}$	$\frac{1}{2}$	$\frac{1}{10}$	$\frac{1}{5}$
100 ml	25 ml			
200 ml			20 ml	
600 ml				
800 ml		400 ml		
1000 ml				200 ml

4 Draw lines on the jug to show:

- $\frac{1}{4}$ full
- $\frac{1}{2}$ full
- $\frac{1}{10}$ full
- $\frac{3}{4}$ full

Write the correct amount of ml next to each line.

1000 ml

5 Last year, Bruce weighed 100 kg.

He now weighs $\frac{1}{4}$ more.

How much does he now weigh?

☐ kg

6 Sophie makes some milkshakes to sell at the school fair.

She makes two different sizes.

A small milkshake is 300 ml and a large milkshake is $\frac{2}{3}$ more.

What is the volume of a large milkshake in ml?

☐ ml

Amelia drinks $\frac{1}{2}$ of a large milkshake.

Sasha drinks $\frac{1}{3}$ of a small milkshake.

Who drinks more? _____

Reasoning with fractions and decimals

Use your knowledge of fractions and decimals to solve these problems.

1

Put these fractions and decimals into the correct boxes.
One has been done for you.

$\frac{3}{4}$ 0.95 $\frac{1}{3}$ 0.25 $\frac{85}{100}$ 0.09

	More than a half	Less than a half
Fraction	$\frac{85}{100}$	
Decimal		

2 Decide if each statement is **true** or **false**.
Put a tick (✔) in the correct column.

	True	False
Decimal numbers are always less than one whole.		
There are ten hundredths in one tenth.		
$\frac{5}{10}$ is equivalent to one half.		
$\frac{1}{4}$ of 2 is 0.5		

3 The two squares below are $\frac{2}{5}$ of a number strip.

Draw the rest of the number strip.

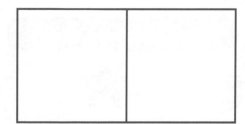

4

James ate $\frac{1}{2}$ a pizza.

Joe ate $\frac{1}{2}$ of what was left.

Gabby ate the rest of the pizza.
Divide the pizza to show the fraction that each person ate.

Write each amount as a decimal.

Joe [ ]   James [ ]   Gabby [ ]

5

Circle the decimals that give an answer of 7 when rounded to the nearest whole number.

7.2   6.8   7.5   6.5   7.7

Fill in the missing words to complete the sentence.

When the tenths number is a _____ or above, the number

rounds _____ .

6

Janie has a set of cars.
It is made up 10 yellow cars, 5 red cars, 1 green car and 4 blue cars.
Write each of these amounts as a fraction of the whole set.

Yellow cars [ ]   Red cars [ ]   Green cars [ ]   Blue cars [ ]

Janie says, "If you take away two yellow cars, you will have to change the fractions for all of the other cars."
Is Janie right? Explain your answer.

_____

_____

_____

How much did you do?   ## Questions 1-6

Circle a star to
show how much
you have done.

Some

Most

All

55

Answers

Fractions

Page 4

1 $\frac{1}{2}$

2 $\frac{1}{2}$ – one half, $\frac{1}{4}$ – one quarter, $\frac{1}{3}$ – one third

3 $\frac{3}{4}, \frac{1}{4}$

   $\frac{3}{5}, \frac{3}{8}$

Page 5

4 $\frac{1}{2}$

5 $\frac{1}{4}$

6 $\frac{4}{8}$ or $\frac{1}{2}$

   $\frac{2}{8}$ or $\frac{1}{4}$

   $\frac{2}{8}$ or $\frac{1}{4}$

Halves and quarters

Page 6

1 Either half (one part) of each shape may be coloured.

2 Any one quarter (one part) of each shape may be coloured.

3 ✗, ✔,
   ✔, ✗

Page 7

4 ✔, ✗,
   ✔, ✔

5 5, 6, 50
   8, 10, 15
   20, 100, 25

6 2, 3, 25
   4, 5, 10
   1, 100, 15

Thirds and fifths

Page 8

1 Any one third (one part) of each shape may be coloured.

2 Any one fifth (one part) of each shape may be coloured.

3 $\frac{2}{6}$ or $\frac{1}{3}$, $\frac{2}{10}$ or $\frac{1}{5}$

   $\frac{3}{9}$ or $\frac{1}{3}$, $\frac{3}{15}$ or $\frac{1}{5}$

Page 9

4 Any three balloons may be coloured.
   Any two party hats may be coloured.

5 1, 3, 2
   5, 10, 4

6 2, 4, 3, 10

Tenths

Page 10

1 ✔, ✗, ✔
   ✗, ✔

2 Four parts should be coloured.
   Seven parts should be coloured.
   Three parts should be coloured.
   Six parts should be coloured.
   Ten parts should be coloured.

3 tennis balls $\frac{2}{10}$ $\left(\text{or } \frac{1}{5}\right)$, footballs $\frac{3}{10}$,

   rugby balls $\frac{4}{10}$ $\left(\text{or } \frac{2}{5}\right)$, cricket balls $\frac{1}{10}$

Page 11

4

5 $\frac{7}{10}, \frac{9}{10}$

   $\frac{3}{10}, \frac{2}{10}, \frac{1}{10}$

   $\frac{8}{10}, \frac{10}{10}$ (accept 1)

6

(number lines with values: 0.2, 0.4, 0.5, 0.6, 0.8; 1.3, 1.4, 1.7, 1.8, 1.9; 2.1, 2.2, 2.3, 2.4, 2.6, 2.7, 2.8, 2.9)

Hundredths

Page 12

1 Seven squares coloured red
   Ten squares coloured orange
   Three squares coloured green
   Five squares coloured blue

2 $\dfrac{5}{100}, \dfrac{24}{100}$

   $\dfrac{81}{100}, \dfrac{48}{100}$

3 **From top to bottom:** $\dfrac{2}{100}, \dfrac{9}{100}, \dfrac{29}{100}, \dfrac{84}{100}$

Page 13

4 $\dfrac{4}{100}, \dfrac{3}{100}$

   $\dfrac{20}{100}, \dfrac{21}{100}$

   $\dfrac{64}{100}, \dfrac{63}{100}$

   $\dfrac{99}{100}, \dfrac{96}{100}$

5 2, 5, 7
   9, 10, 4

6 $\dfrac{1}{100}$ of £1, $\dfrac{2}{100}$ (or $\dfrac{1}{50}$) of £1, $\dfrac{5}{100}$ (or $\dfrac{1}{20}$) of £1

   $\dfrac{10}{100}$ (or $\dfrac{1}{10}$) of £1, $\dfrac{20}{100}$ (or $\dfrac{1}{5}$) of £1,

   $\dfrac{50}{100}$ (or $\dfrac{1}{2}$) of £1

Unit fractions

Page 14

1 $\dfrac{1}{2}$ – one half, $\dfrac{1}{4}$ – one quarter,

   $\dfrac{1}{5}$ – one fifth, $\dfrac{1}{8}$ – one eighth,

   $\dfrac{1}{10}$ – one tenth

2 **From top to bottom:** $\dfrac{1}{2}, \dfrac{1}{4}, \dfrac{1}{7}, \dfrac{1}{10}$

3 **From top to bottom:** $\dfrac{1}{5}, \dfrac{1}{8}$

Page 15

4   $\dfrac{1}{9}$ $\dfrac{1}{10}$

    $\dfrac{1}{6}$ $\dfrac{1}{5}$

   $\dfrac{1}{8}$

5

$\dfrac{1}{2}$								$\dfrac{1}{2}$	
$\dfrac{1}{3}$			$\dfrac{1}{3}$			$\dfrac{1}{3}$			
$\dfrac{1}{4}$		$\dfrac{1}{4}$		$\dfrac{1}{4}$		$\dfrac{1}{4}$			
$\dfrac{1}{5}$	$\dfrac{1}{5}$	$\dfrac{1}{5}$	$\dfrac{1}{5}$	$\dfrac{1}{5}$					
$\dfrac{1}{6}$	$\dfrac{1}{6}$	$\dfrac{1}{6}$	$\dfrac{1}{6}$	$\dfrac{1}{6}$	$\dfrac{1}{6}$				
$\dfrac{1}{7}$	$\dfrac{1}{7}$	$\dfrac{1}{7}$	$\dfrac{1}{7}$	$\dfrac{1}{7}$	$\dfrac{1}{7}$	$\dfrac{1}{7}$			
$\dfrac{1}{8}$	$\dfrac{1}{8}$	$\dfrac{1}{8}$	$\dfrac{1}{8}$	$\dfrac{1}{8}$	$\dfrac{1}{8}$	$\dfrac{1}{8}$	$\dfrac{1}{8}$		
$\dfrac{1}{9}$	$\dfrac{1}{9}$	$\dfrac{1}{9}$	$\dfrac{1}{9}$	$\dfrac{1}{9}$	$\dfrac{1}{9}$	$\dfrac{1}{9}$	$\dfrac{1}{9}$	$\dfrac{1}{9}$	
$\dfrac{1}{10}$	$\dfrac{1}{10}$	$\dfrac{1}{10}$	$\dfrac{1}{10}$	$\dfrac{1}{10}$	$\dfrac{1}{10}$	$\dfrac{1}{10}$	$\dfrac{1}{10}$	$\dfrac{1}{10}$	$\dfrac{1}{10}$

Non-unit fractions

Page 16

1 **These fractions should be circled:**
$\frac{3}{4}, \frac{2}{5}, \frac{4}{6}, \frac{3}{10}$

2 **From top to bottom:** $\frac{2}{5}, \frac{4}{10}$ (or $\frac{2}{5}$), $\frac{7}{8}$,
$\frac{4}{6}$ (or $\frac{2}{3}$), $\frac{10}{12}$ (or $\frac{5}{6}$)

3 Oranges $\frac{2}{10}$ (or $\frac{1}{5}$), Apples $\frac{3}{10}$,
Pears $\frac{1}{10}$, Bananas $\frac{4}{10}$ (or $\frac{2}{5}$)

Page 17

4 Three parts should be coloured.
Six parts should be coloured.
Three parts should be coloured.
Five parts should be coloured.
Five parts should be coloured.

5 $\frac{9}{10}, \frac{7}{8}, \frac{4}{5}$
$\frac{2}{3}, \frac{5}{6}, \frac{99}{100}$

6 £6, £9
£12, £15, £24

Comparing fractions

Page 18

1 $\frac{3}{4} > \frac{2}{4}$ (or $\frac{1}{2}$) or $\frac{1}{4}$
$\frac{3}{6}$ (or $\frac{1}{2}$) $> \frac{2}{6}$ (or $\frac{1}{3}$) or $\frac{1}{6}$

2 $\frac{1}{4} < \frac{2}{4}$ (or $\frac{1}{2}$)
$\frac{6}{10} > \frac{5}{10}$ (or $\frac{1}{2}$)

3 **The following fractions should be ticked:**
$\frac{1}{2}, \frac{1}{8}$
$\frac{1}{3}, \frac{2}{6}$
$\frac{1}{100}, \frac{3}{6}$

Page 19

4 <, <
>, <
>, >

5 **The following fractions should be**
circled: $\frac{7}{10}, \frac{3}{4}, \frac{6}{8}, \frac{40}{100}$

6 ✔, ✗
✔, ✗
✔, ✗
✗, ✔

Ordering fractions

Page 20

1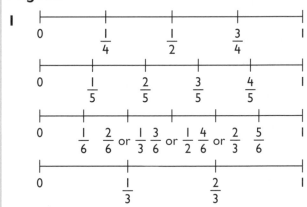

2 $\frac{2}{5}, \frac{3}{5}, \frac{4}{5}$
$\frac{6}{10}, \frac{9}{10}, \frac{10}{10}$
$\frac{2}{100}, \frac{9}{100}, \frac{19}{100}$
$\frac{1}{4}, \frac{3}{4}, \frac{4}{4}$

Page 21

3

Place	Player
1st (most goals)	Bracken
2nd	Paul
3rd	Josh
4th	Mandeep
5th	Sam

4 $\frac{7}{10}$ of a packet of sweets
$\frac{4}{5}$ of a carton of juice

5 (Carla) John, Ben, Sophie, Alex, Grace,
Keith, Jess

Fraction word problems

Page 22

1 8 (pink), 16 (yellow)

2 5 (brown), 20 (white), 7 (male), 7 (female)

3 Stanley and Rachel

Page 23

4 £3, £2.50, Ben

5 £50, £20, £30

6

Pet	Number of votes
Guinea pig	10
Fish	6
Rabbit	3
Hamster	5
Dog	6

Guinea pig

Fractions equivalent to one half

Page 24

1 ✔, ✗
   ✔, ✗
   ✔, ✔

2 $\frac{4}{8}$ (4 parts coloured), $\frac{3}{6}$ (3 parts coloured)

   $\frac{6}{12}$ (6 parts coloured), $\frac{5}{10}$ (5 parts coloured)

3 **The following fractions should be circled:** $\frac{4}{8}, \frac{5}{10}, \frac{10}{20}$

Page 25

4 $\frac{2}{6}$, ✗

   $\frac{10}{20}$, ✔

5 $\frac{3}{6}, \frac{2}{4}, \frac{5}{10}, \frac{6}{12}, \frac{10}{20}, \frac{50}{100}, \frac{3}{6}$

6 $\frac{6}{12} = \frac{1}{2}$

   $\frac{6}{10} > \frac{1}{2}$

Fraction families

Page 26

1 $\frac{1}{5} = \frac{2}{10}, \frac{4}{16} = \frac{2}{8}$

   $\frac{2}{3} = \frac{4}{6}$

2 Two parts coloured = four parts coloured, two parts coloured = four parts coloured, eight parts coloured = four parts coloured

3 $\frac{1}{5}, \frac{1}{3}, \frac{1}{4}, \frac{1}{3}$

Page 27

4 $\frac{2}{5} = \frac{4}{10} = \frac{6}{15} = \frac{8}{20}, \frac{3}{5} = \frac{6}{10} = \frac{9}{15} = \frac{12}{20}$

5 **Answers may vary.**

   $\frac{1}{2} = \frac{2}{4} = \frac{4}{8} = \frac{5}{10} = \frac{6}{12} = \frac{10}{20}$

   $\frac{1}{3} = \frac{2}{6} = \frac{4}{12} = \frac{5}{15}$

   $\frac{1}{4} = \frac{2}{8} = \frac{3}{12} = \frac{5}{20}$

   $\frac{1}{5} = \frac{2}{10} = \frac{3}{15} = \frac{4}{20}$

   $\frac{1}{6} = \frac{2}{12}$

   $\frac{1}{10} = \frac{2}{20}$

Adding fractions

Page 28

1 $\frac{2}{4} + \frac{1}{4} = \frac{3}{4}$

   $\frac{3}{9} + \frac{6}{9} = \frac{9}{9}, \frac{2}{8} + \frac{4}{8} = \frac{6}{8}$ $\left(\text{accept } \frac{1}{4} + \frac{2}{4} = \frac{3}{4}\right)$

2 $\frac{3}{4}, \frac{4}{5}$

   $\frac{3}{3}, \frac{5}{6}$

   $\frac{8}{10}, \frac{32}{100}$

3 **Accept equivalent fractions:**

$\frac{2}{4}\left(\text{or } \frac{1}{2}\right), \frac{3}{5}, \frac{4}{10}$

$\frac{3}{6}, \frac{3}{8}, \frac{22}{100}$

Page 29

4 $\frac{1}{3} + \frac{1}{3} = \frac{2}{3}$

$\frac{2}{5} + \frac{2}{5} = \frac{4}{5}$

$\frac{1}{2} + \frac{1}{2} = 1$

$\frac{3}{8} + \frac{2}{8} = \frac{5}{8}$

5 $\frac{3}{4}, \frac{4}{5}$

$\frac{4}{8}\left(\text{or } \frac{1}{2}\right), \frac{2}{9}$

$\frac{1}{8}$ and $\frac{5}{8}$ or $\frac{2}{8}$ and $\frac{4}{8}$ or $\frac{3}{8}$ and $\frac{3}{8}$ or $\frac{1}{4}$ and $\frac{2}{4}$

(pairs of answers may be given in any order)

6 **The following fractions should be circled:** $\frac{2}{9}, \frac{1}{9}$ and $\frac{4}{9}$

Subtracting fractions

Page 30

1 $\frac{12}{12} - \frac{6}{12} = \frac{6}{12}$

$\frac{6}{9} - \frac{3}{9} = \frac{3}{9}$

$\frac{6}{8} - \frac{1}{8} = \frac{5}{8}$

$\frac{5}{6} - \frac{3}{6} = \frac{2}{6}$

2 **Accept equivalent fractions:**

$\frac{1}{4}, \frac{0}{5}$ (or 0), $\frac{1}{3}$

$\frac{3}{6}\left(\text{or } \frac{1}{2}\right), \frac{6}{10}, \frac{14}{100}$

3 $\frac{2}{4}\left(\text{or } \frac{1}{2}\right), \frac{2}{5}, \frac{5}{10}$

$\frac{1}{6}, \frac{3}{8}, \frac{0}{100}$ (or 0)

Page 31

4 $\frac{3}{3} - \frac{1}{3} = \frac{2}{3}$

$\frac{4}{5} - \frac{2}{5} = \frac{2}{5}$

$\frac{1}{2} - \frac{1}{2} = 0$

$\frac{3}{8} - \frac{2}{8} = \frac{1}{8}$

5 $\frac{5}{8} - \frac{3}{8} = \frac{2}{8}$ or $\frac{5}{8} - \frac{2}{8} = \frac{3}{8}$

$\frac{7}{8} - \frac{1}{8} = \frac{6}{8}$ or $\frac{7}{8} - \frac{6}{8} = \frac{1}{8}$

6 $\frac{2}{5}$

Decimal and fraction equivalents 1

Page 32

1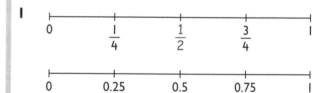

2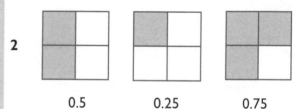

0.5   0.25   0.75

3 $\frac{1}{2}$, 0.5

$\frac{1}{4}$, 0.25

$\frac{3}{4}$, 0.75

Page 33

4 $\frac{3}{4}\left(\text{or } \frac{6}{8}\right)$, 0.75

$\frac{1}{2}\left(\text{or } \frac{4}{8}\right)$, 0.5

$\frac{1}{4}\left(\text{or } \frac{2}{8}\right)$, 0.25

5 $\frac{6}{8}\left(\text{or } \frac{3}{4}\right)$, 0.25

6 $\frac{1}{4}$, 0.25

    $\frac{8}{16}$ $\left(\text{or } \frac{1}{2}\right)$, 0.5

Decimal and fraction equivalents 2

Page 34

1 0.5, 0.6, 0.4, 0.3
    0.1, 0.8, 0.7, 0.9

2 Six parts should be coloured.
    Six parts should be coloured.
    Eight parts should be coloured.
    Eight parts should be coloured.

3 $0.3 = \frac{3}{10}$, $0.9 = \frac{9}{10}$, $0.4 = \frac{4}{10}$, $0.7 = \frac{7}{10}$

Page 35

4 0.3, 0.7, 0.2, $\frac{5}{10}$

    0.6, $\frac{2}{10}$, $\frac{9}{10}$, 0.8

5 0.13, 0.17, 0.28, 0.07
    0.94, 0.22, 0.06, 0.09
    $\frac{93}{100}$, $\frac{15}{100}$, $\frac{71}{100}$, $\frac{26}{100}$
    $\frac{91}{100}$, $\frac{4}{100}$, $\frac{38}{100}$, $\frac{9}{100}$

6 14 squares coloured red, 16 squares
    coloured blue
    9 squares coloured red, 11 squares
    coloured blue

Counting with decimals

Page 36

1
    (or 7.0)

2 5.1, 5.2, 5.3, 5.4, 5.5, 5.6
    4.7, 4.8, 4.9, 5.0, 5.1, 5.2

3 4.4, 4.3, 4.2
    2.8, 2.7, 2.6
    5.9, 5.8, 5.7
    9.0 (or 9), 8.9, 8.8
    10.1, 10.0 (or 10), 9.9

Page 37

4
    (or 7.0 or 7)

5 4.61, 4.62, 4.63, 4.64, 4.65, 4.66
    2.97, 2.98, 2.99, 3.00, 3.01, 3.02

6 3.13, 3.12, 3.11
    2.06, 2.05, 2.04
    0.98, 0.97, 0.96
    4.99, 4.98, 4.97
    10.88, 10.87, 10.86

Dividing whole numbers by ten

Page 38

1 Rings should be drawn to show ten groups of
    four sweets.
    40, 4, 40 ÷ 10 = 4

2 8.0
    2.0, 1.0

3 30 ÷ 10 = 3, 70 ÷ 10 = 7
    90 ÷ 10 = 9, 50 ÷ 10 = 5
    120 ÷ 10 = 12, 100 ÷ 10 = 10

Page 39

4 **From top to bottom:** 2.2, 4.8, 9.6

5 42 ÷ 10 = 4.2, 55 ÷ 10 = 5.5
    29 ÷ 10 = 2.9, 67 ÷ 10 = 6.7
    99 ÷ 10 = 9.9, 82 ÷ 10 = 8.2

6 96 ÷ 10 = 9.6 cm

Dividing whole numbers by one hundred

Page 40

1. 9 (in ones column) or 9.00
   8 (in ones columns) or 8.00

2. 4 (in ones column) or 4.00
   2 (in ones column) or 2.00

3. $1000 \div 100 = 10$, $700 \div 100 = 7$
   $500 \div 100 = 5$, $300 \div 100 = 3$
   $600 \div 100 = 6$, $1200 \div 100 = 12$

Page 41

4. **From top to bottom:** 5.63, 1.24, 9.69

5. $242 \div 100 = 2.42$, $555 \div 100 = 5.55$
   $629 \div 100 = 6.29$, $467 \div 100 = 4.67$
   $899 \div 100 = 8.99$, $347 \div 100 = 3.47$

6. £5.97
   £1.45
   £7.42

Decimals and money

Page 42

1. £3.80

2. £3.20

3. £47 (or £47.00)

Page 43

4. £8.50

5. £8.53

6. £16.72

Rounding decimals

Page 44

1. **From top to bottom:** 2, 3, 8

2. **From top to bottom:** 1, 3, 5, 10

3.

Results	Act	Actual Score
1st place	Eastlife	7.5
2nd place	Jessie G	7.1
3rd place	All Directions	6.6
4th place	Big Mix	5.9

Page 45

4. **From top to bottom:** true, false, true, false

5. 25
   $1 + 4 = 5$
   $10 \times 10 = 100$
   $98 - 16 = 82$

6. 1 kg, 2 kg, 2 kg
   $((1 \times 50p) + (2 \times 40p) + (2 \times 50p)) = £2.30$

Comparing decimals

Page 46

1. **The following decimals should be circled:** 4.6, 3.9, 1.5, 7.9

2. $6.3 < 6.5$, $4.8 > 4.4$
   $2.9 > 2.7$, $6.2 < 6.4$
   $8.2 < 8.5$, $5.7 > 5.4$

3. **The following decimals should be ticked:** 2.25, 4.66, 3.10, 5.60

Page 47

4. $2.21 < 2.32$, $4.65 < 4.68$
   $7.12 > 7.09$, $6.32 < 6.35$
   $5.12 < 5.17$, $8.64 > 8.46$

5. false, true
   true, true
   false, true
   true, true
   false, true

6. 6.00, 6.06, 6.60, 6.61
   2.00, 2.20, 2.22, 2.50
   4.05, 4.57, 4.59, 4.60
   7.00, 7.17, 7.70, 7.71

Decimals and measurement

Page 48

1. 8.4 cm

2. 161.1 cm

3. 50.3 cm

Page 49

4. 300.45 miles

5. 120.8 cm

6. 60.13 cm

Decimal problems

Page 50

1
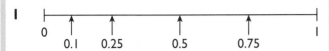

2 95p, £1.20, £4.97, £4.99

3 5 + 0.6 + 0.04
7 + 0.6 + 0.03
9 + 0.9 + 0.02
10 + 2 + 0.2 + 0.09

Page 51

4 7.2, 10.8
1.3, 2.2
5, 4.5

5 6.2, 0.8
2.5, 3.2
7.0, 9.8

6 3.2 + 2.1 = 5.3 or 2.1 + 3.2 = 5.3 or
3.1 + 2.4 = 5.5 or 2.4 + 3.1 = 5.5
5.5 − 2.4 = 3.1 or 5.5 − 3.1 = 2.4 or
5.3 − 2.1 = 3.2 or 5.3 − 3.2 = 2.1

Fractions and measurement

Page 52

1 80 cm

2 York 10°C, Glasgow 2°C,
Newquay 5°C

3

	$\frac{1}{4}$	$\frac{1}{2}$	$\frac{1}{10}$	$\frac{1}{5}$
100 ml	25 ml	50 ml	10 ml	20 ml
200 ml	50 ml	100 ml	20 ml	40 ml
600 ml	150 ml	300 ml	60 ml	120 ml
800 ml	200 ml	400 ml	80 ml	160 ml
1000 ml	250 ml	500 ml	100 ml	200 ml

Page 53

4

5 125 kg

6 500 ml, Amelia

Reasoning with fractions and decimals

Page 54

1

	More than a half		Less than a half	
Fraction	$\frac{85}{100}$	$\frac{3}{4}$	$\frac{1}{3}$	
Decimal	0.95		0.25	0.09

2 **From top to bottom:** false, true, true, true

3 Three squares should be added to the strip.

Page 55

4 Pizza divided to show one half and two
quarters.
James 0.5, Joe 0.25, Gabby 0.25

5 **The following numbers should be circled:**
7.2, 6.8, 6.5
When the tenths number is a **five** or above,
the number rounds **up**.

6 Yellow cars $\frac{10}{20}$ or $\frac{1}{2}$, Red cars $\frac{5}{20}$ or $\frac{1}{4}$

Green cars $\frac{1}{20}$, Blue cars $\frac{4}{20}$ or $\frac{1}{5}$

Yes, because the denominator will change as
well (from 20 to 18).

Check your progress

- Shade in the stars on the progress certificate to show how much you did. Shade one star for every ⭐ you circled in this book.

- If you have shaded fewer than 20 stars, go back to the pages where you circled Some ☆ or Most ⭐ and try those pages again.

- If you have shaded 20 or more stars, well done!

✂ -

Collins Easy Learning Fractions and decimals bumper book Ages 7-9

Progress certificate

to

Name _____   Date _____

pages 4–5	pages 6–7	pages 8–9	pages 10–11	pages 12–13	pages 14–15	pages 16–17	pages 18–19	pages 20–21
☆ 1	☆ 2	☆ 3	☆ 4	☆ 5	☆ 6	☆ 7	☆ 8	☆ 9

pages 22–23	pages 24–25	pages 26–27	pages 28–29	pages 30–31	pages 32–33	pages 34–35	pages 36–37	pages 38–39
☆ 10	☆ 11	☆ 12	☆ 13	☆ 14	☆ 15	☆ 16	☆ 17	☆ 18

pages 40–41	pages 42–43	pages 44–45	pages 46–47	pages 48–49	pages 50–51	pages 52–53	pages 54–55
☆ 19	☆ 20	☆ 21	☆ 22	☆ 23	☆ 24	☆ 25	☆ 26